© Charles and Stacey Matthews, June 2011

All Rights Reserved.

Notice:

Composers, arrangers, lyricists, editors and publishers are entitled to fair payment for their work, and it is both unfair and illegal to threaten their livelihoods by unauthorized copying. We kindly request your cooperation.

**Lyrics taken from Scriptures from the Holy Bible,
New International Version ®, NIV®
Copyright © 1973, 1978, 1984, 2011 by Biblica, Inc.
TM Used by permission.
All rights reserved worldwide.**

International Standard Book Number: 978-0-9895619-0-7

How Majestic Is Your Word: Scripture Memory Songs For Children

Psalm 119
1 Thessalonians 5:15
Ephesians 6:1-4

Dedicated to our precious children:

Makira, John, Megan, Madeline,
Jaydon, Melinda, Jed, Mandy and
any others the Lord should so graciously give us.

Much Love Always,

Mom & Dad

Table of Contents

Verses   Pages

1. Psalm 119: 1-8 | א Aleph | Blessed Are They...   1-3
2. Psalm 119: 9-16 | ב Beth | How Can A Young Man...   4-6
3. Psalm 119: 17-24 | ג Gimel | Do Good To Your Servant...   7-10
4. Psalm 119: 25-32 | ד Daleth | I Am Laid Low...   11-14
5. Psalm 119: 33-40 | ה He | Teach Me...   15-18
6. Psalm 119: 41-48 | ו Waw | May Your Unfailing Love...   19-22
7. Psalm 119: 49-56 | ז Zayin | Remember Your Word...   23-26
8. Psalm 119: 57-64 | ח Heth | You Are My Portion...   27-29
9. Psalm 119: 65-72 | ט Teth | Do Good To Your Servant According To...   30-33
10. Psalm 119: 73-80 | י Yodh | Your Hands Made Me...   34-38
11. Psalm 119: 81-88 | כ Kaph | My Soul Faints...   39-42
12. Psalm 119: 89-96 | ל Lamedh | Your Word...   43-46
13. Psalm 119: 97-104 | מ Mem | Oh, How I Love Your Law...   47-50
14. Psalm 119: 105-112 | נ Nun | Your Word Is A Lamp...   51-53
15. Psalm 119: 113-120 | ס Samekh | I Hate Double-Minded Men...   54-57
16. Psalm 119: 121-128 | ע Ayin | I Have Done...   58-61
17. Psalm 119: 129-136 | פ Pe | Your Statues Are Wonderful...   62-65
18. Psalm 119: 137-144 | צ Tsadhe | Righteous Are You...   66-69
19. Psalm 119: 145-152 | ק Qoph | I Call With All My Heart...   70-73
20. Psalm 119: 153-160 | ר Resh | Look Upon My Suffering...   74-77
21. Psalm 119: 161-168 | ש Sin and Shin | Rulers Persecute Me...   78-81
22. Psalm 119: 169-176 | ת Taw | May My Cry...   82-86
23. Ephesians 6:1-4 | Children Obey Your Parents...   87-91
24. 1 Thessalonians 5:15 | Make Sure...   92

Blessed Are They
א Aleph
Psalm 119:1-8

Arrangement
Mark Rice

Composers: Charles and Stacey Matthews

© Charles and Stacey Matthews, June 2011, All Rights Reserved.
Lyrics taken from Scriptures from the Holy Bible, New International Version ®,
NIV® Copyright © 1973, 1978, 1984, 2011 by Biblica, Inc. TM
Used by permission. All rights reserved worldwide.

How Can A Young Man Keep His Way Pure?

ב Beth
Psalm 119: 9-16

Arrangement
Mandee Sikich

Composers
Charles and Stacey Matthews

© Charles and Stacey Matthews, June 2011, All Rights Reserved. Lyrics taken from Scriptures from
the Holy Bible, New International Version ®, NIV®
Copyright © 1973, 1978, 1984, 2011 by Biblica, Inc. TM
Used by permission. All rights reserved worldwide.

Do Good to Your Servant
ג Gimel
Psalm 119: 17-24

Arrangement
Mandee Sikich

Composers
Charles and Stacey Matthews

© Charles and Stacey Matthews, June 2011, All Rights Reserved. Lyrics taken from Scriptures from
the Holy Bible, New International Version ®, NIV®
Copyright © 1973, 1978, 1984, 2011 by Biblica, Inc. TM
Used by permission. All rights reserved worldwide.

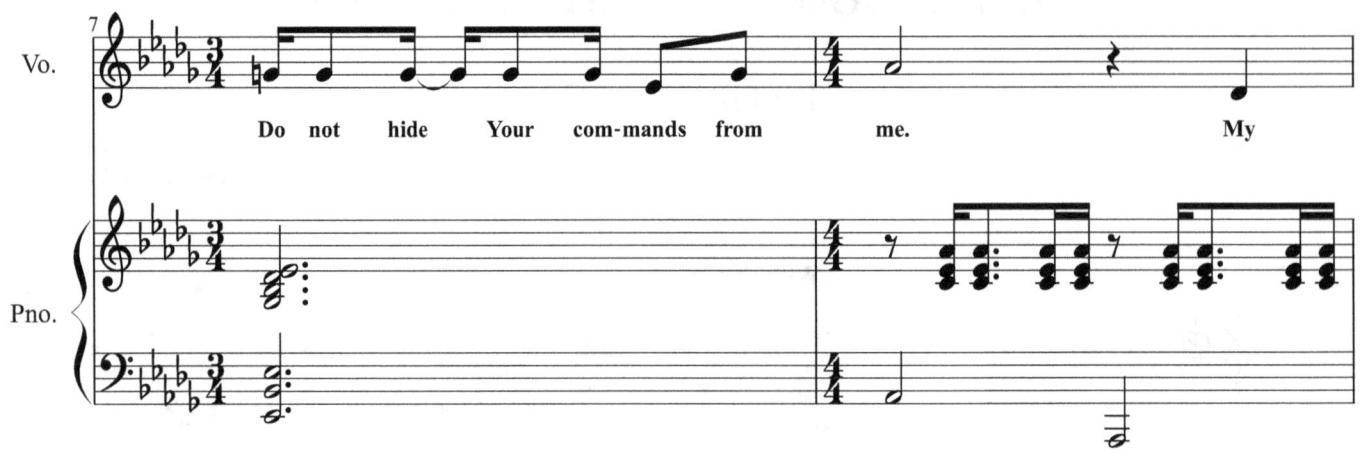

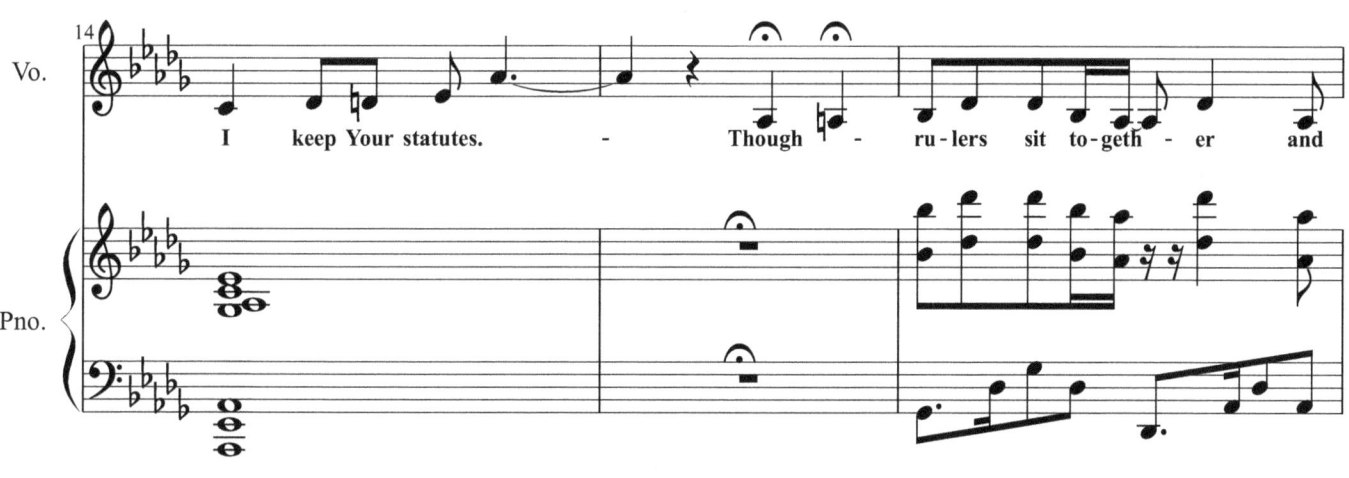

I Am Laid Low In The Dust
ד Daleth
Psalm 119: 25-32

Arrangement
Mandee Sikich

Composers
Charles and Stacey Matthews

© Charles and Stacey Matthews, June 2011, All Rights Reserved. Lyrics taken from Scriptures from
the Holy Bible, New International Version ®, NIV®
Copyright © 1973, 1978, 1984, 2011 by Biblica, Inc. TM
Used by permission. All rights reserved worldwide.

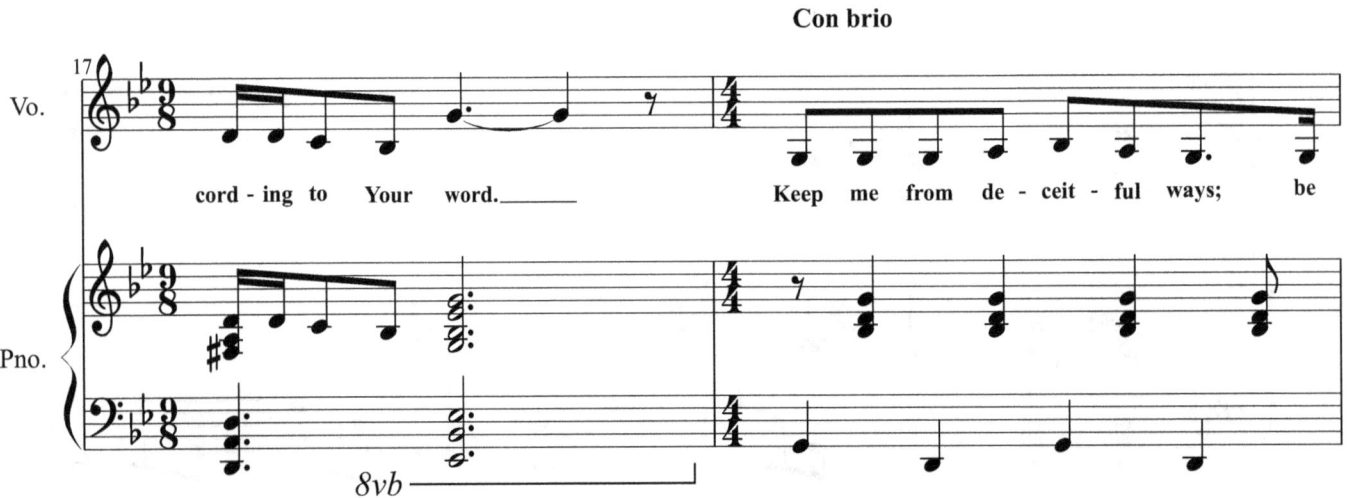

© Charles and Stacey Matthews, June 2011, All Rights Reserved. Lyrics taken from Scriptures from
the Holy Bible, New International Version ®, NIV®
Copyright © 1973, 1978, 1984, 2011 by Biblica, Inc. TM
Used by permission. All rights reserved worldwide.

© Charles and Stacey Matthews, June 2011, All Rights Reserved. Lyrics taken from Scriptures from
the Holy Bible, New International Version ®, NIV®
Copyright © 1973, 1978, 1984, 2011 by Biblica, Inc. TM
Used by permission. All rights reserved worldwide.

Teach Me, O Lord
ה He
Psalm 119: 33-40

Arrangement
Mandee Sikich

Composers
Charles and Stacey Matthews

© Charles and Stacey Matthews, June 2011, All Rights Reserved. Lyrics taken from Scriptures from
the Holy Bible, New International Version ®, NIV®
Copyright © 1973, 1978, 1984, 2011 by Biblica, Inc. TM
Used by permission. All rights reserved worldwide.

17

May Your Unfailing Love
ו Waw
Psalm 119: 41-48

Arrangement
Mandee Sikich

Composers
Charles and Stacey Matthews

© Charles and Stacey Matthews, June 2011, All Rights Reserved. Lyrics taken from Scriptures from
the Holy Bible, New International Version ®, NIV®
Copyright © 1973, 1978, 1984, 2011 by Biblica, Inc. TM
Used by permission. All rights reserved worldwide.

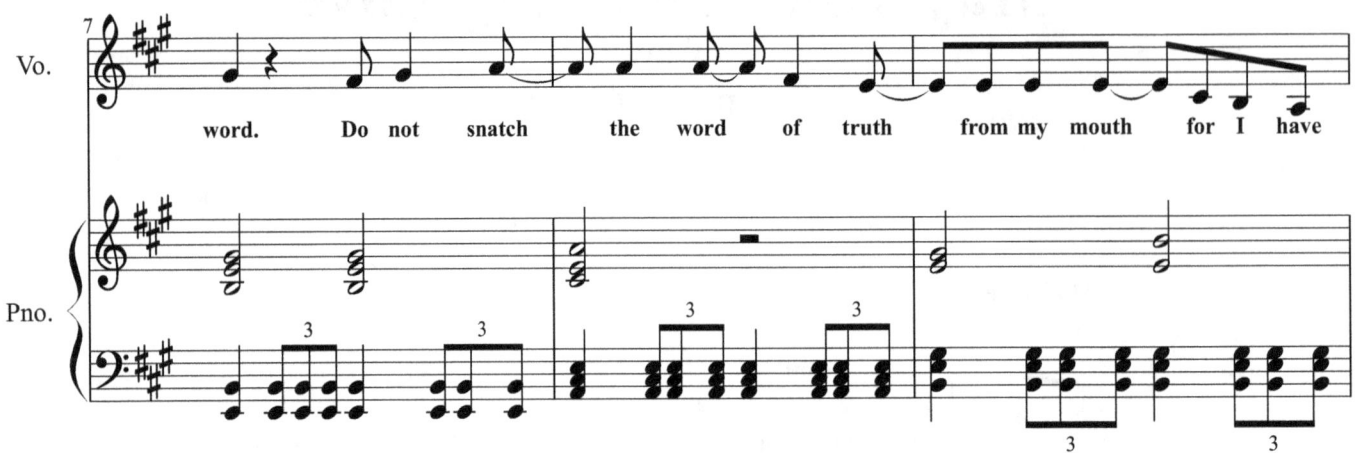

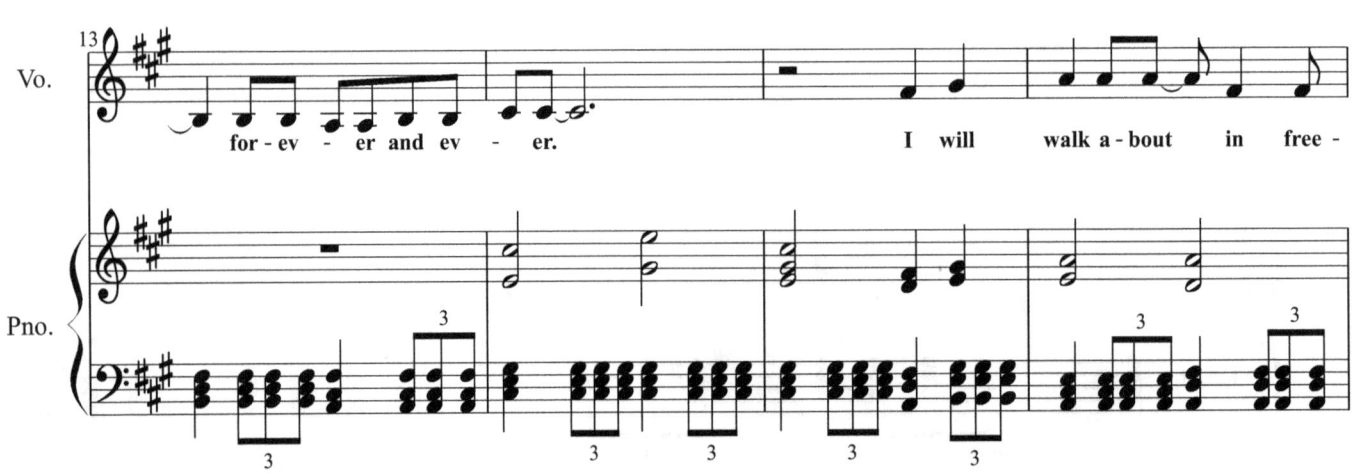

© Charles and Stacey Matthews, June 2011, All Rights Reserved. Lyrics taken from Scriptures from
the Holy Bible, New International Version ®, NIV®
Copyright © 1973, 1978, 1984, 2011 by Biblica, Inc. TM
Used by permission. All rights reserved worldwide.

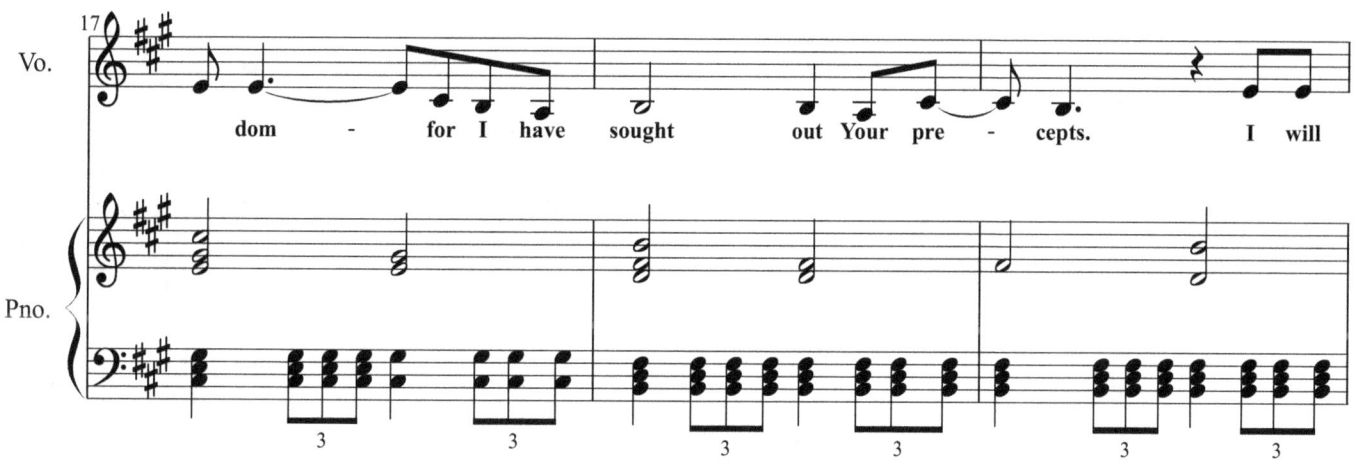
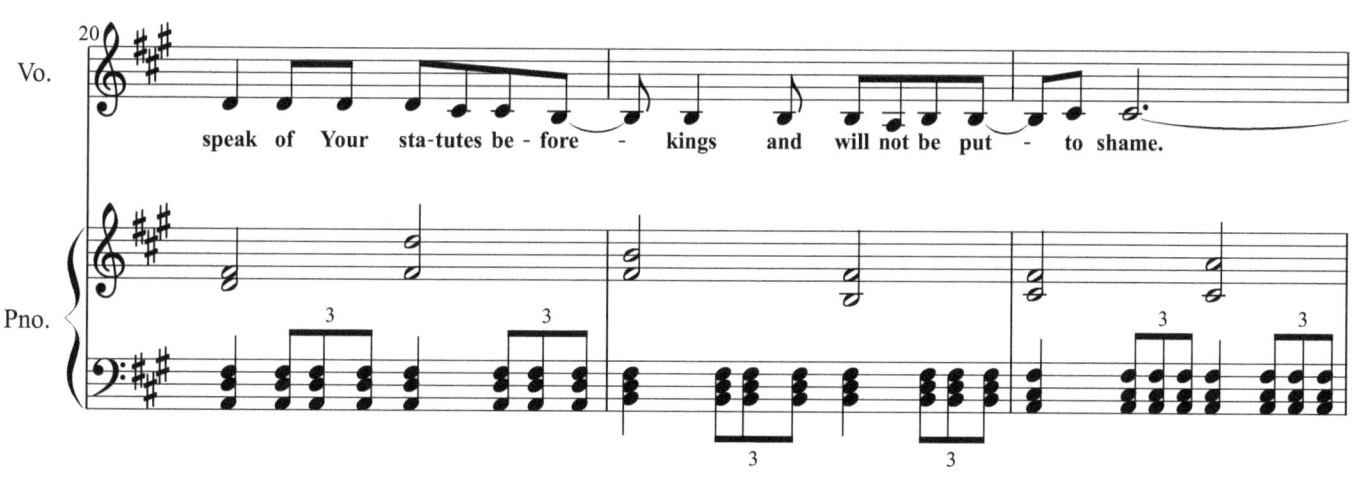

© Charles and Stacey Matthews, June 2011, All Rights Reserved. Lyrics taken from Scriptures from
the Holy Bible, New International Version ®, NIV®
Copyright © 1973, 1978, 1984, 2011 by Biblica, Inc. TM
Used by permission. All rights reserved worldwide.

Remember Your Word to Your Servant
ז Zayin
Psalm 119: 49-56

Arrangement
Mandee Sikich

Composers
Charles and Stacey Matthews

© Charles and Stacey Matthews, June 2011, All Rights Reserved. Lyrics taken from Scriptures from
the Holy Bible, New International Version ®, NIV®
Copyright © 1973, 1978, 1984, 2011 by Biblica, Inc. TM
Used by permission. All rights reserved worldwide.

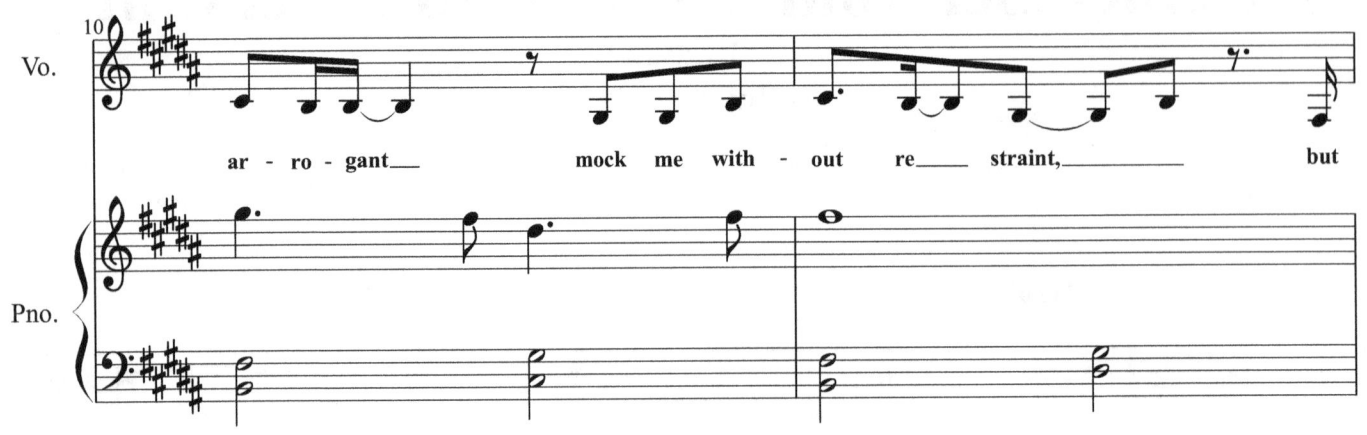

25

You Are My Portion, O Lord

ח Heth
Psalm 119: 57-64

Arrangement
Mandee Sikich

Composers
Charles and Stacey Matthews

© Charles and Stacey Matthews, June 2011, All Rights Reserved. Lyrics taken from Scriptures from
the Holy Bible, New International Version ®, NIV®
Copyright © 1973, 1978, 1984, 2011 by Biblica, Inc. TM
Used by permission. All rights reserved worldwide.

© Charles and Stacey Matthews, June 2011, All Rights Reserved. Lyrics taken from Scriptures from
the Holy Bible, New International Version ®, NIV®
Copyright © 1973, 1978, 1984, 2011 by Biblica, Inc. TM
Used by permission. All rights reserved worldwide.

Do Good To Your Servant

ט Teth
Psalm 119: 65-72

Arrangement
Mandee Sikich

Composers
Charles and Stacey Matthews

© Charles and Stacey Matthews, June 2011, All Rights Reserved. Lyrics taken from Scriptures from
the Holy Bible, New International Version ®, NIV®
Copyright © 1973, 1978, 1984, 2011 by Biblica, Inc. TM
Used by permission. All rights reserved worldwide.

© Charles and Stacey Matthews, June 2011, All Rights Reserved. Lyrics taken from Scriptures from the Holy Bible, New International Version ®, NIV®
Copyright © 1973, 1978, 1984, 2011 by Biblica, Inc. TM
Used by permission. All rights reserved worldwide.

Your Hands Made Me
’ Yodh
Psalm 119: 73-80

Arrangement
Mandee Sikich

Composers
Charles and Stacey Matthews

© Charles and Stacey Matthews, June 2011, All Rights Reserved. Lyrics taken from Scriptures from
the Holy Bible, New International Version ®, NIV®
Copyright © 1973, 1978, 1984, 2011 by Biblica, Inc. TM
Used by permission. All rights reserved worldwide.

35

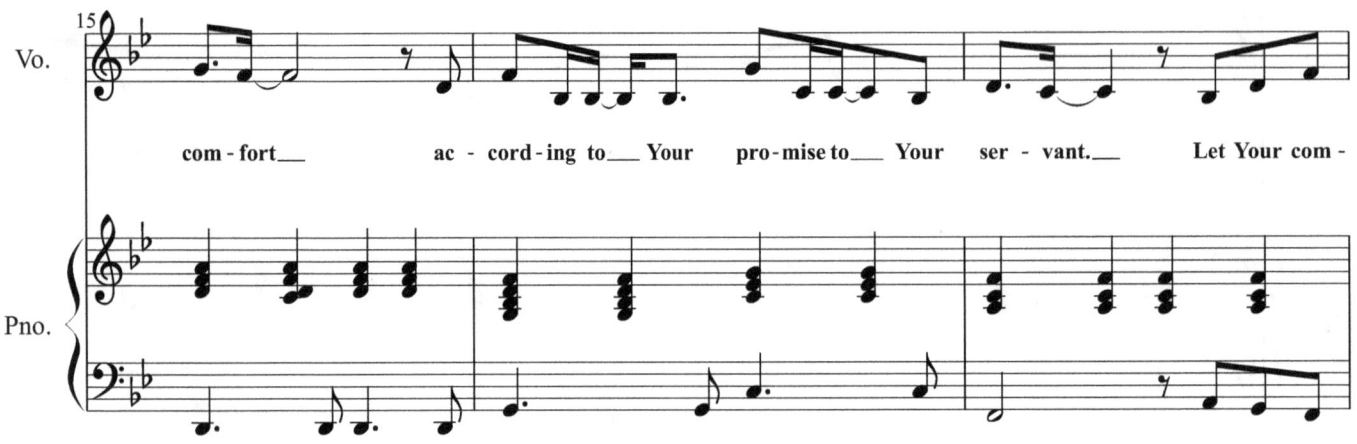

© Charles and Stacey Matthews, June 2011, All Rights Reserved. Lyrics taken from Scriptures from
the Holy Bible, New International Version ®, NIV®
Copyright © 1973, 1978, 1984, 2011 by Biblica, Inc. TM
Used by permission. All rights reserved worldwide.

My Soul Faints with Longing
כ Kaph
Psalm 119: 81-88

Arrangement
Mandee Sikich

Composers
Charles and Stacey Matthews

© Charles and Stacey Matthews, June 2011, All Rights Reserved. Lyrics taken from Scriptures from
the Holy Bible, New International Version ®, NIV®
Copyright © 1973, 1978, 1984, 2011 by Biblica, Inc. TM
Used by permission. All rights reserved worldwide.

Your Word, O Lord, Is Eternal
ל Lamedh
Psalm 119: 89-96

Arrangement
Mandee Sikich

Composers
Charles and Stacey Matthews

© Charles and Stacey Matthews, June 2011, All Rights Reserved. Lyrics taken from Scriptures from
the Holy Bible, New International Version ®, NIV®
Copyright © 1973, 1978, 1984, 2011 by Biblica, Inc. TM
Used by permission. All rights reserved worldwide.

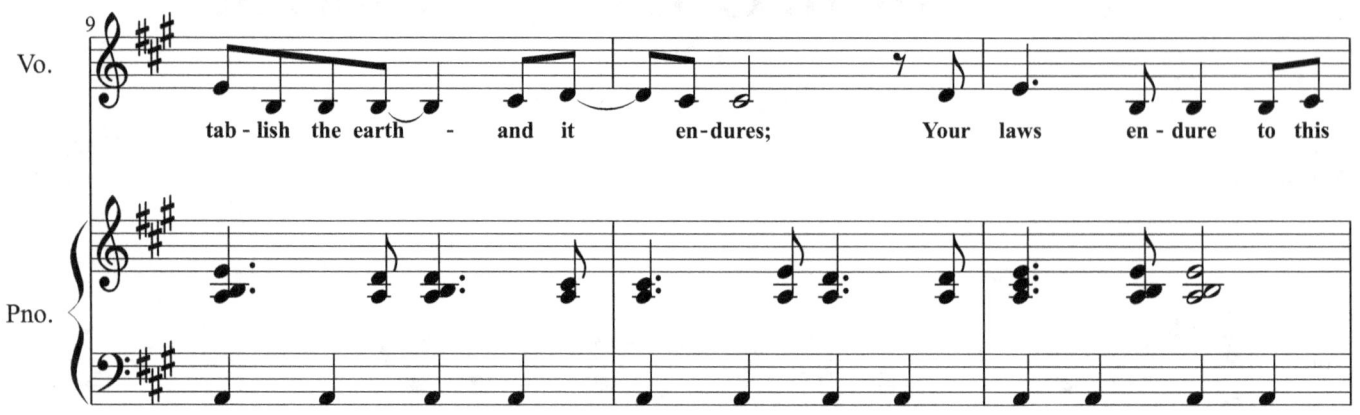

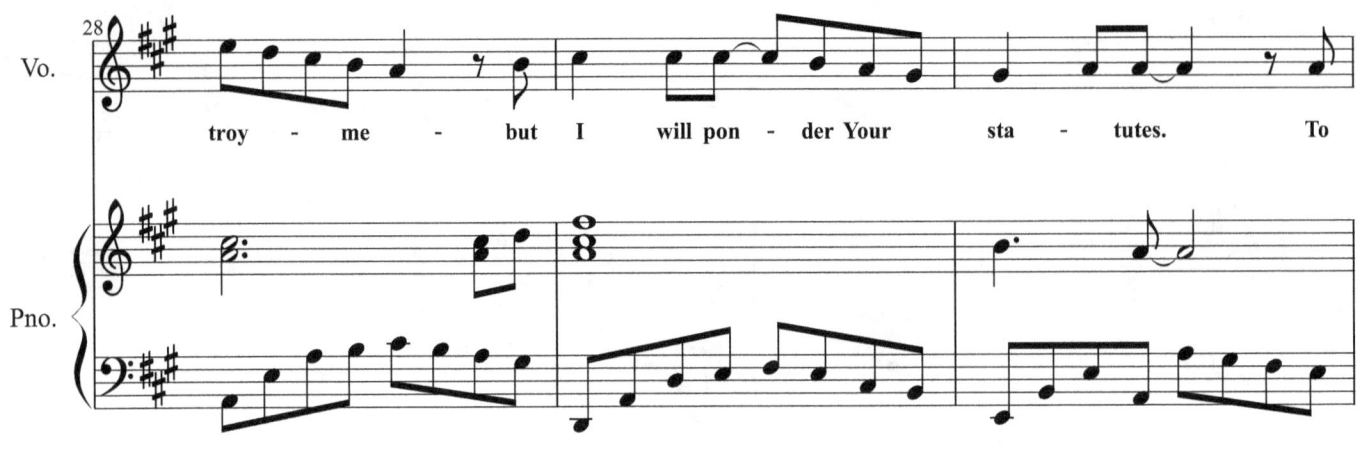

© Charles and Stacey Matthews, June 2011, All Rights Reserved. Lyrics taken from Scriptures from
the Holy Bible, New International Version ®, NIV®
Copyright © 1973, 1978, 1984, 2011 by Biblica, Inc. TM
Used by permission. All rights reserved worldwide.

O How I Love Your Law
מ Mem
Psalm 119: 97-104

Arrangement
Mandee Sikich

Composers
Charles and Stacey Matthews

© Charles and Stacey Matthews, June 2011, All Rights Reserved. Lyrics taken from Scriptures from
the Holy Bible, New International Version ®, NIV®
Copyright © 1973, 1978, 1984, 2011 by Biblica, Inc. TM
Used by permission. All rights reserved worldwide.

Your Word Is A Lamp To My Feet

׆ Nun
Psalm 119: 105-112

Arrangement
Mandee Sikich

Composers
Charles and Stacey Matthews

© Charles and Stacey Matthews, June 2011, All Rights Reserved. Lyrics taken from Scriptures from
the Holy Bible, New International Version ®, NIV®
Copyright © 1973, 1978, 1984, 2011 by Biblica, Inc. TM
Used by permission. All rights reserved worldwide.

I Hate Double-Minded Men
ס Samekh
Psalm 119: 113-120

Arrangement
Mandee Sikich

Composers
Charles and Stacey Matthews

© Charles and Stacey Matthews, June 2011, All Rights Reserved. Lyrics taken from Scriptures from
the Holy Bible, New International Version ®, NIV®
Copyright © 1973, 1978, 1984, 2011 by Biblica, Inc. TM
Used by permission. All rights reserved worldwide.

55

I Have Done What is Righteous

ע Ayin
Psalm 119: 121-128

Arrangement
Mandee Sikich

Composers
Charles and Stacey Matthews

© Charles and Stacey Matthews, June 2011, All Rights Reserved. Lyrics taken from Scriptures from
the Holy Bible, New International Version ®, NIV®
Copyright © 1973, 1978, 1984, 2011 by Biblica, Inc. TM
Used by permission. All rights reserved worldwide.

Your Statutes are Wonderful

פ Pe
Psalm 119: 129-136

Arrangement
Mandee Sikich

Composers
Charles and Stacey Matthews

© Charles and Stacey Matthews, June 2011, All Rights Reserved. Lyrics taken from Scriptures from
the Holy Bible, New International Version ®, NIV®
Copyright © 1973, 1978, 1984, 2011 by Biblica, Inc. TM
Used by permission. All rights reserved worldwide.

Righteous Are You, O Lord
צ Tsadhe
Psalm 119: 137-144

Arrangement
Mandee Sikich

Composers
Charles and Stacey Matthews

© Charles and Stacey Matthews, June 2011, All Rights Reserved. Lyrics taken from Scriptures from
the Holy Bible, New International Version ®, NIV®
Copyright © 1973, 1978, 1984, 2011 by Biblica, Inc. TM
Used by permission. All rights reserved worldwide.

67

I Call With All My Heart
ק Qoph
Psalm 119: 145-152

Arrangement
Mandee Sikich

Composers
Charles and Stacey Matthews

© Charles and Stacey Matthews, June 2011, All Rights Reserved. Lyrics taken from Scriptures from
the Holy Bible, New International Version ®, NIV®
Copyright © 1973, 1978, 1984, 2011 by Biblica, Inc. TM
Used by permission. All rights reserved worldwide.

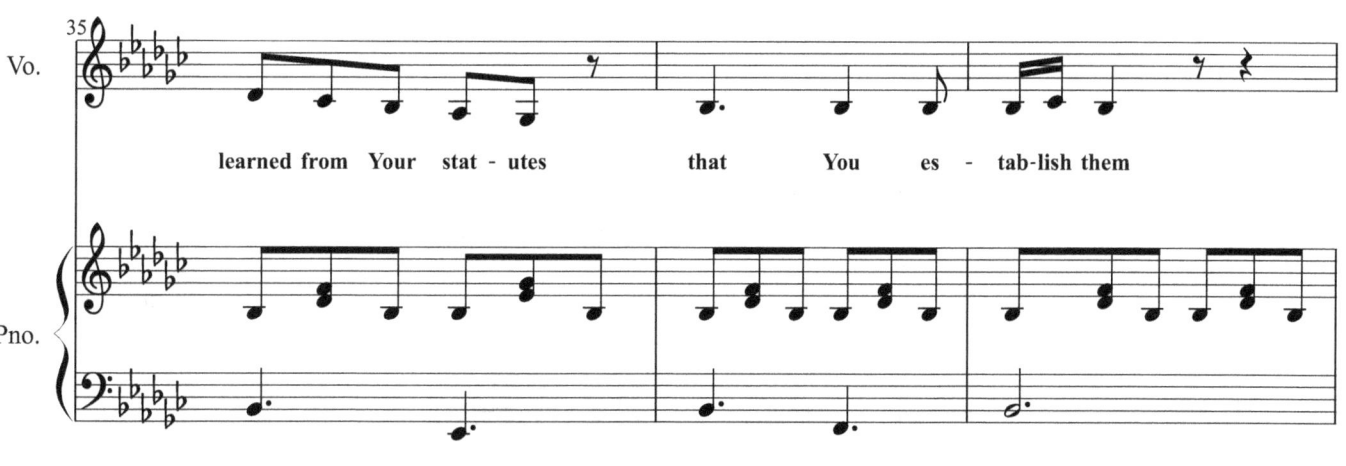

Look Upon My Suffering
ר Resh
Psalm 119: 153-160

Arrangement
Mandee Sikich

Composers
Charles and Stacey Matthews

© Charles and Stacey Matthews, June 2011, All Rights Reserved. Lyrics taken from Scriptures from
the Holy Bible, New International Version ®, NIV®
Copyright © 1973, 1978, 1984, 2011 by Biblica, Inc. TM
Used by permission. All rights reserved worldwide.

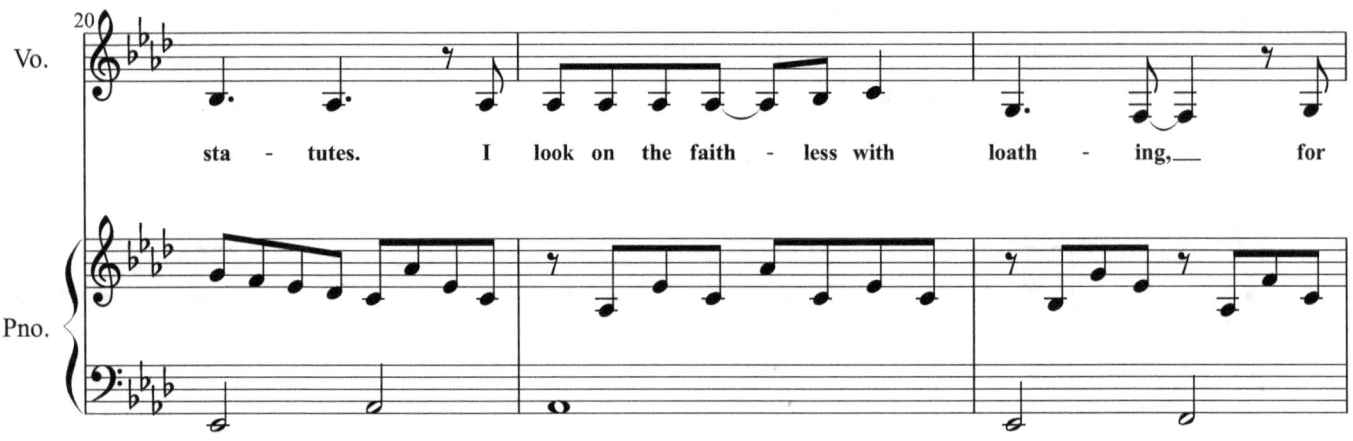

Rulers Persecute Me Without Cause

ש Sin and Shin
Psalm 119: 161-168

Arrangement
Mandee Sikich

Composers
Charles and Stacey Matthews

© Charles and Stacey Matthews, June 2011, All Rights Reserved. Lyrics taken from Scriptures from
the Holy Bible, New International Version ®, NIV®
Copyright © 1973, 1978, 1984, 2011 by Biblica, Inc. TM
Used by permission. All rights reserved worldwide.

79

May My Cry Come Before You, O Lord

ת Taw
Psalm 119: 169-176

Arrangement
Mandee Sikich

Composers
Charles and Stacey Matthews

© Charles and Stacey Matthews, June 2011, All Rights Reserved. Lyrics taken from Scriptures from
the Holy Bible, New International Version ®, NIV®
Copyright © 1973, 1978, 1984, 2011 by Biblica, Inc. TM
Used by permission. All rights reserved worldwide.

83

© Charles and Stacey Matthews, June 2011, All Rights Reserved. Lyrics taken from Scriptures from
the Holy Bible, New International Version ®, NIV®
Copyright © 1973, 1978, 1984, 2011 by Biblica, Inc. TM
Used by permission. All rights reserved worldwide.

Children, Obey Your Parents/ Honor Your Father And Mother

Arrangement
Mandee Sikich

Ephesians 6:1-4

Composers
Charles and Stacey Matthews

© Charles and Stacey Matthews, June 2011, All Rights Reserved. Lyrics taken from Scriptures from
the Holy Bible, New International Version ®, NIV®
Copyright © 1973, 1978, 1984, 2011 by Biblica, Inc. TM
Used by permission. All rights reserved worldwide.

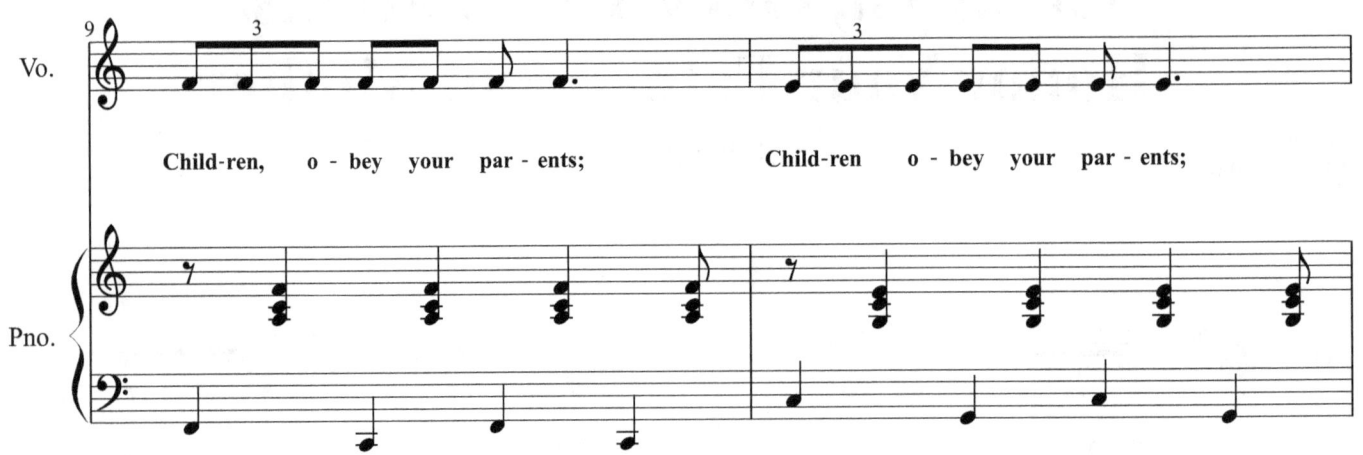

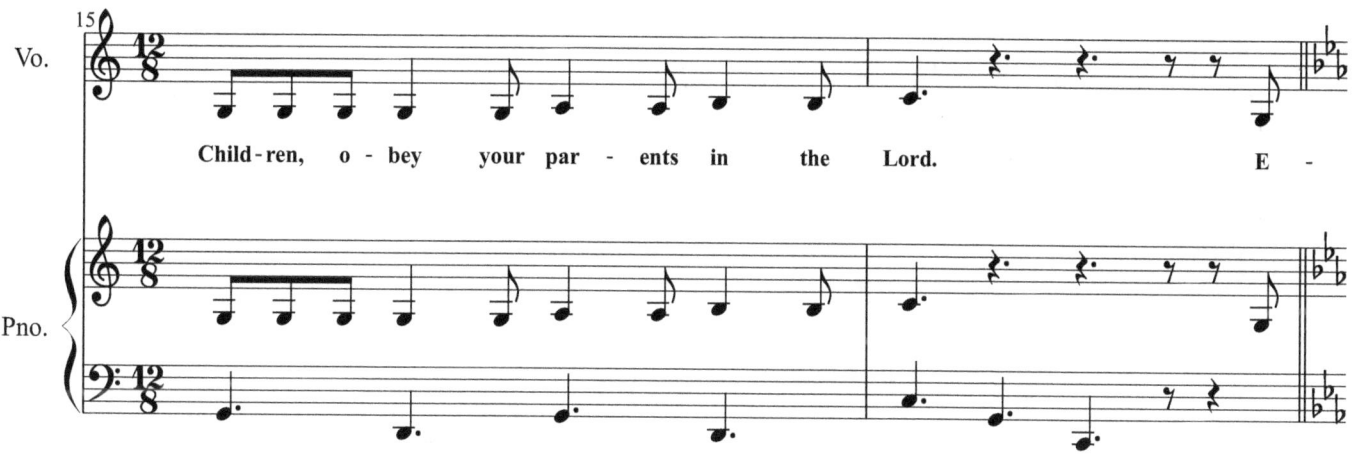

Make Sure
I Thessalonians 5:15

Arrangement
Mandee Sikich

Composers
Charles and Stacey Matthews

© Charles and Stacey Matthews, June 2011, All Rights Reserved. Lyrics taken from Scriptures from the Holy Bible, New International Version ®, NIV®
Copyright © 1973, 1978, 1984, 2011 by Biblica, Inc. TM
Used by permission. All rights reserved worldwide.

www.ingramcontent.com/pod-product-compliance
Lightning Source LLC
Chambersburg PA
CBHW081016040426
42444CB00014B/3238